POPULAR SONGS

HAL LEONARD
STUDENT PIANO LIBRARY

Christmas at the Piano

Eight Easy Holiday Favorites

Arranged by Lynda Lybeck-Robinson

CONTENTS

T0088544

ISBN 978-1-5400-5792-1

HAL•LEONARD®

For all works contained herein:
Unauthorized copying, arranging, adapting, recording, Internet posting, public performance,
or other distribution of the music in this publication is an infringement of copyright.
Infringers are liable under the law.

Visit Hal Leonard Online at
www.halleonard.com

Contact us:
Hal Leonard
7777 West Bluemound Road
Milwaukee, WI 53213
Email: info@halleonard.com

In Europe, contact:
Hal Leonard Europe Limited
42 Wigmore Street
Marylebone, London, W1U 2RN
Email: info@halleonardeurope.com

In Australia, contact:
Hal Leonard Australia Pty. Ltd.
4 Lentara Court
Cheltenham, Victoria, 3192 Australia
Email: info@halleonard.com.au

Believe

from Warner Bros. Pictures' THE POLAR EXPRESS

Words and Music by Glen Ballard
and Alan Silvestri
Arranged by Lynda Lybeck-Robinson

Copyright © 2004 Joblana Music, Universal Music Corp., Hazen Music and Arlovol Music
All Rights on behalf of Joblana Music Administered by Sony/ATV Music Publishing LLC, 424 Church Street, Suite 1200, Nashville, TN 37219
All Rights on behalf of Hazen Music Administered by Universal Music Corp.
All Rights on behalf of Arlovol Music Administered by Penny Farthing Music c/o Concord Music Publishing
International Copyright Secured   All Rights Reserved

but one by one, we ___
trust - ing star - light ___

all had to grow ___ up.
to get where they need to be.

When it seems the mag-ic's slipped a -
When it seems that we have lost our

mf

way, we find it all a - gain on Christ-mas Day.
way, we find our-selves a - gain on Christ-mas Day.

Be -

lieve in what your heart is say-ing, hear the mel - o - dy that's play-ing. There's no time to waste, there's so

much to cel - e - brate. Be - lieve in what you feel in - side and give your dreams the wings to

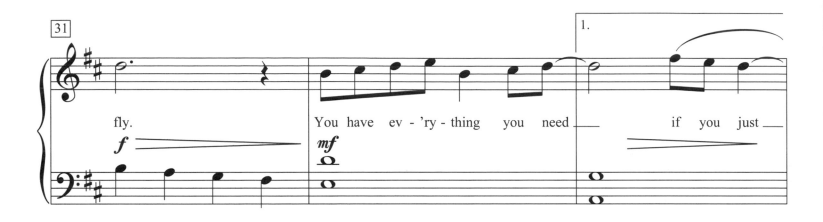

fly. You have ev - 'ry - thing you need ___ if you just ___

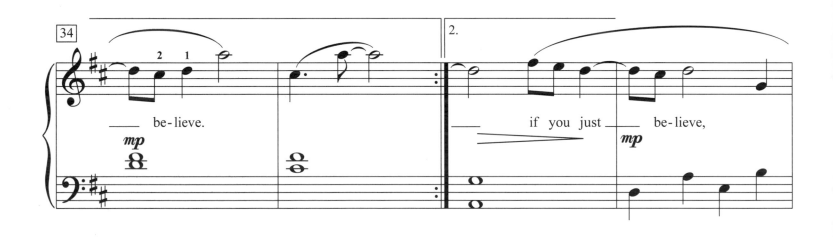

___ be - lieve. if you just ___ be - lieve,

if you just ___ be - lieve, just be - lieve.

4

Breath of Heaven
(Mary's Song)

Words and Music by Amy Grant
and Chris Eaton
Arranged by Lynda Lybeck-Robinson

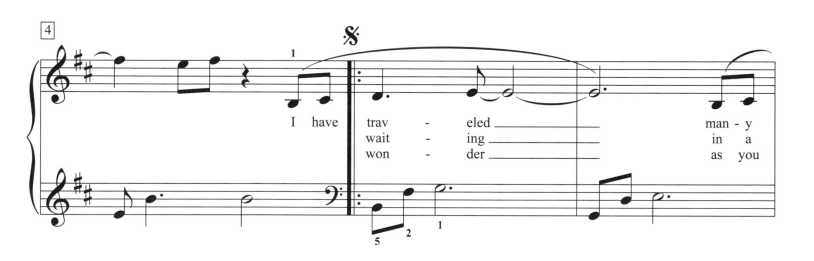

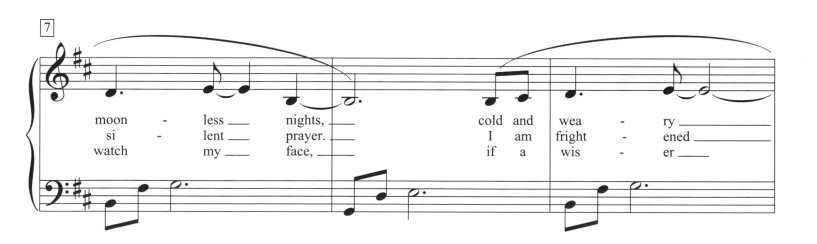

Copyright © 1992, 1997 Clouseau Music, Age To Age Music, Inc. and Riverstone Music, Inc.
All Rights for Clouseau Music Administered by BMG Rights Management (US) LLC
All Rights for Age to Age Music, Inc. and Riverstone Music, Inc. Administered by Music Services
All Rights Reserved   Used by Permission

car - ry Your Son.

I am lone?

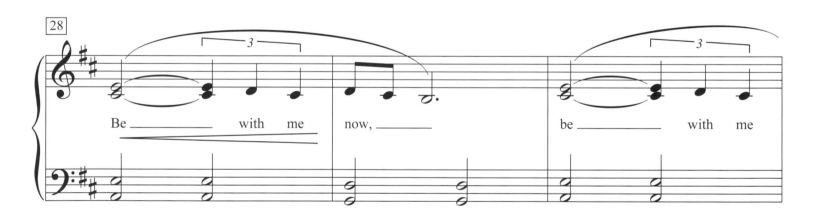

Be _____ with me now, _____ be _____ with me

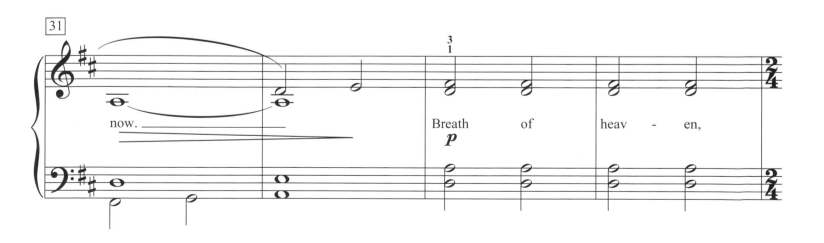

now. _____ Breath of heav - en,

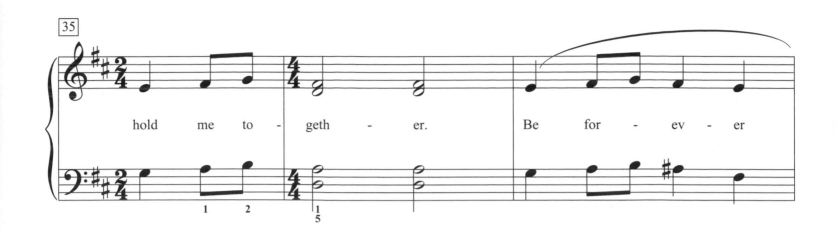

hold me to - geth - er. Be for - ev - er

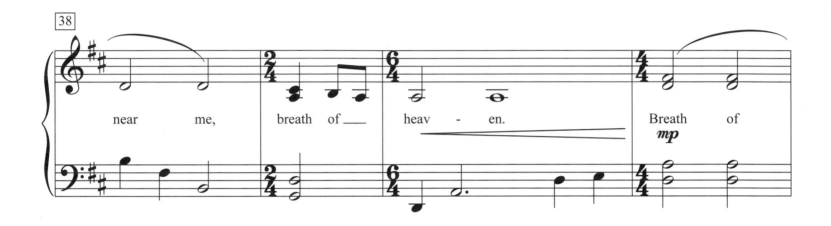

near me, breath of ___ heav - en. Breath of

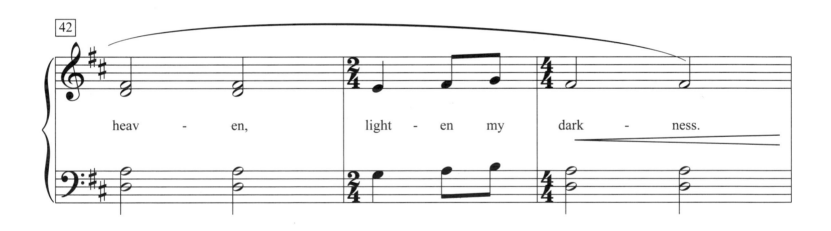

heav - en, light - en my dark - ness.

Pour o - ver me Your ho - li - ness, for You are

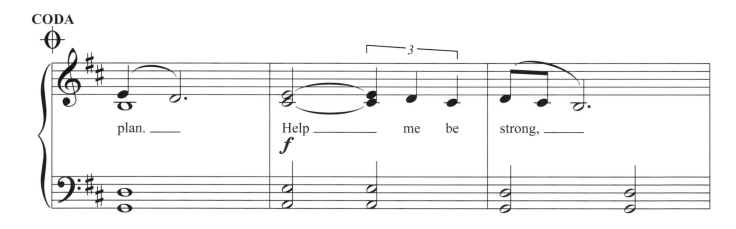

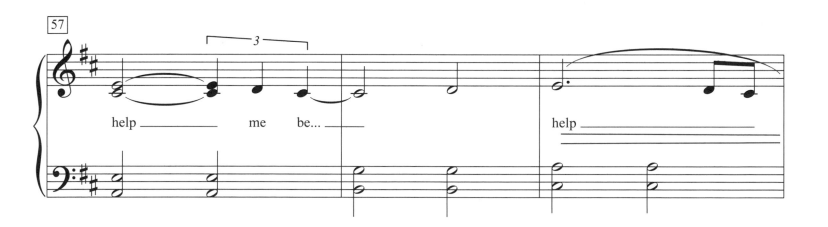

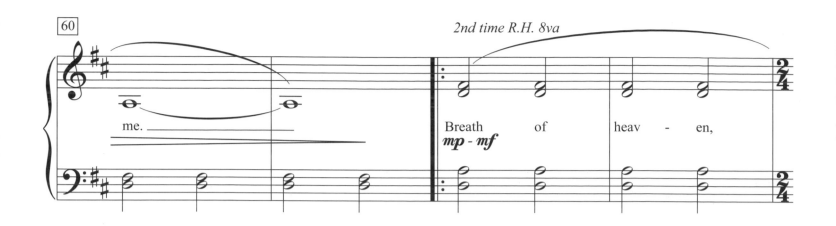

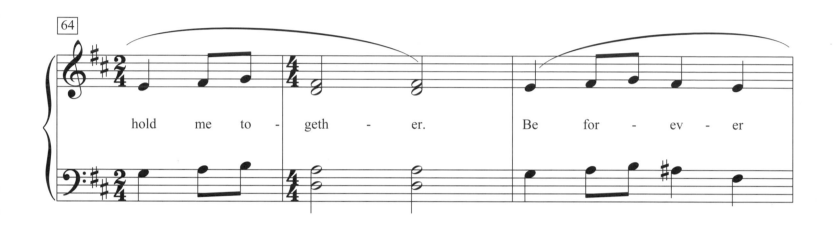

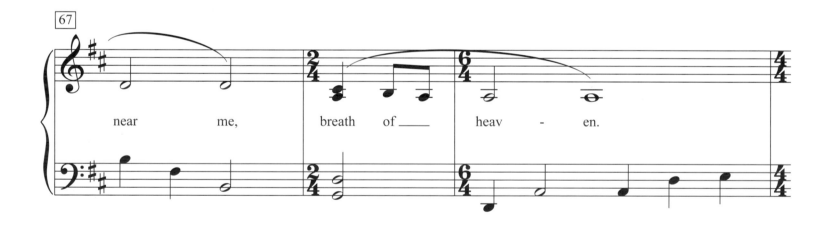

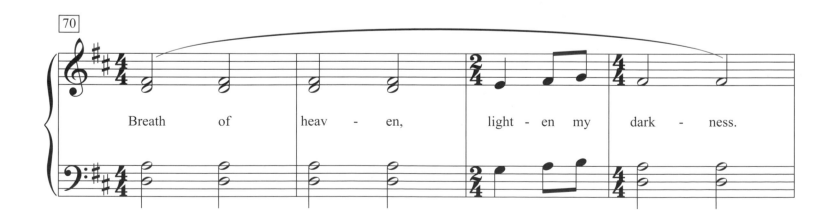

Pour o - ver me Your ho - li - ness, for You are

ho - ly.

ho - ly,

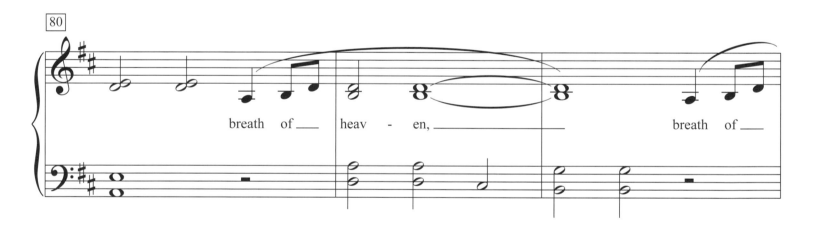

breath of heav - en, breath of

heav - en, breath of heav - en.

rit. *p*

Feliz Navidad

Music and Lyrics by
José Feliciano
Arranged by Lynda Lybeck-Robinson

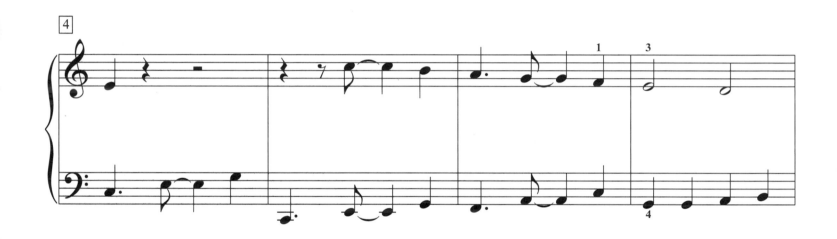

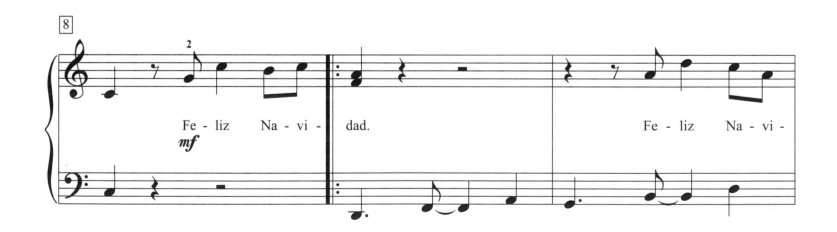

Fe - liz   Na - vi - dad.   Fe - liz   Na - vi -

Copyright © 1970 J & H Publishing Company
Copyright Renewed
All Rights Administered by BMG Rights Management (US) LLC
All Rights Reserved   Used by Permission

dad.   Fe - liz   Na - vi -   dad.   Prós - pe - ro   a -

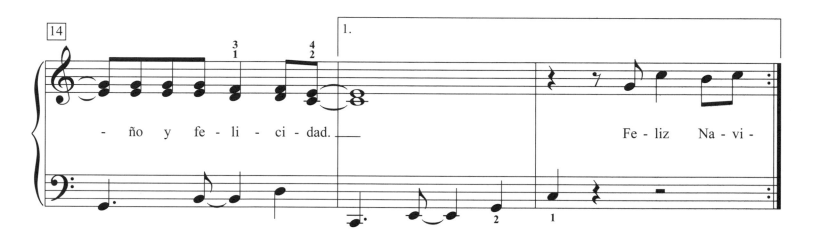

- ño   y   fe - li - ci - dad.   Fe - liz   Na - vi -

I   wan - na   wish   you   a   Mer - ry   Christ - mas

f

with   lots   of   pres - ents   to   make   you   hap - py.   I   wan - na   wish   you   a

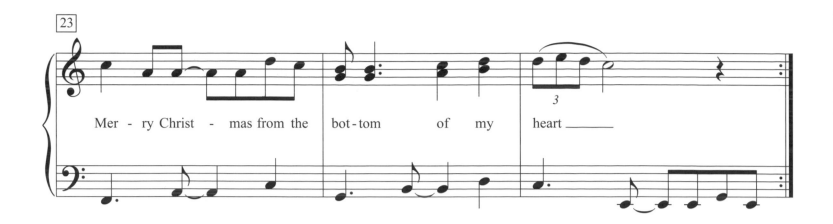

Mer - ry Christ - mas from the bot - tom of my heart _____

Fe - liz Na - vi - dad.

Fe - liz Na - vi -

dad.

Fe - liz Na - vi - dad. Prós - pe - ro a -

- ño y fe - li - ci - dad _____

A Holly Jolly Christmas

Music and Lyrics by
Johnny Marks
Arranged by Lynda Lybeck-Robinson

Moderate Swing (♩ = 132)

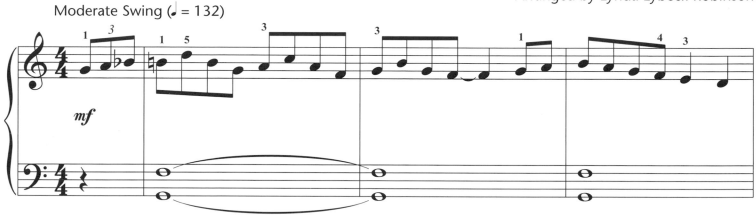

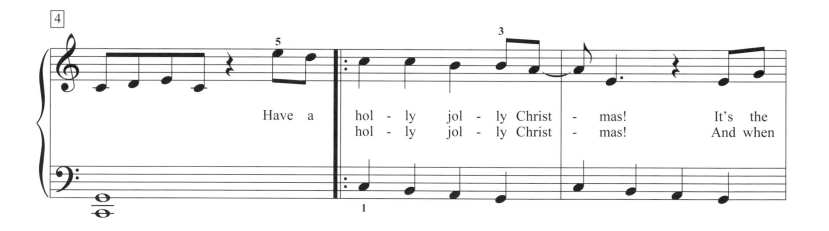

Have a hol - ly jol - ly Christ - mas! It's the
hol - ly jol - ly Christ - mas! And when

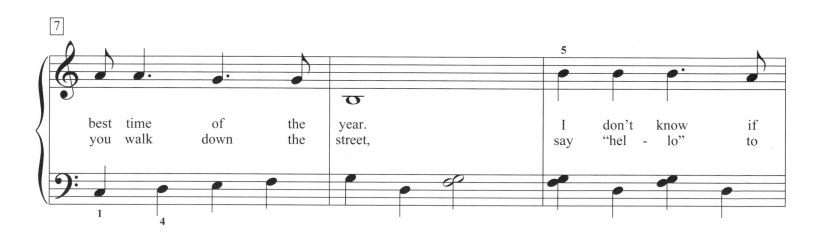

best time of the year. I don't know if
you walk down the street, say "hel - lo" to

Copyright © 1962, 1964 (Renewed 1990, 1992) St. Nicholas Music Inc., 254 W. 54th Street, 12th Floor, New York, New York 10019
All Rights Reserved

there'll be snow, _ but have a cup _ of cheer. Have a
friends you know, _ and

ev - 'ry - one you meet. Ho ho, the

mis - tle - toe, hung where you can see. Some - bod - y

waits for you; kiss her once for me. Have a

16

hol - ly   jol - ly Christ - mas!   And in   case   you   did - n't

hear   oh   by   gol - ly have   a   hol - ly   jol - ly

Christ - mas   this   year!

17

I Wonder as I Wander

By John Jacob Niles
Arranged by Lynda Lybeck-Robinson

Copyright © 1934 (Renewed) by G. Schirmer, Inc. (ASCAP), New York, NY
International Copyright Secured   All Rights Reserved
Reprinted by Permission

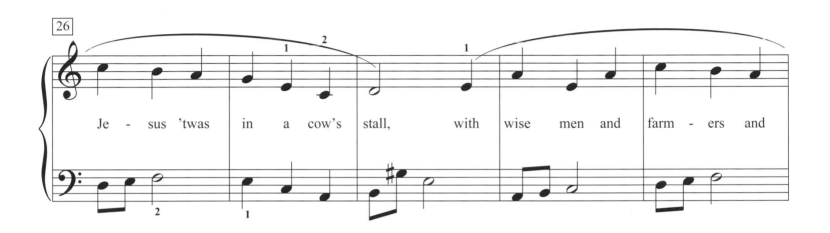

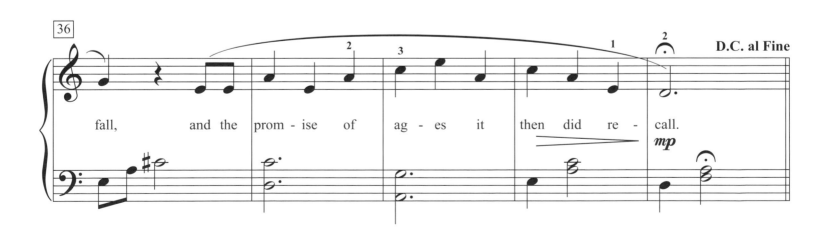

19

The Little Drummer Boy

Words and Music by Harry Simeone,
Henry Onorati and Katherine Davis
Arranged by Lynda Lybeck-Robinson

© 1958 (Renewed) EMI MILLS MUSIC, INC. and INTERNATIONAL KORWIN CORP.
Worldwide Print Rights Administered by ALFRED MUSIC
All Rights Reserved   Used by Permission

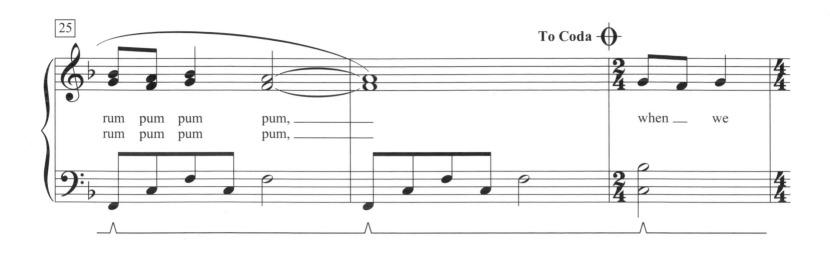

To Coda ⊕

rum pum pum pum, ____
rum pum pum pum, ____

when __ we

come.

rit.

mp a tempo

simile

Lit - tle

mf

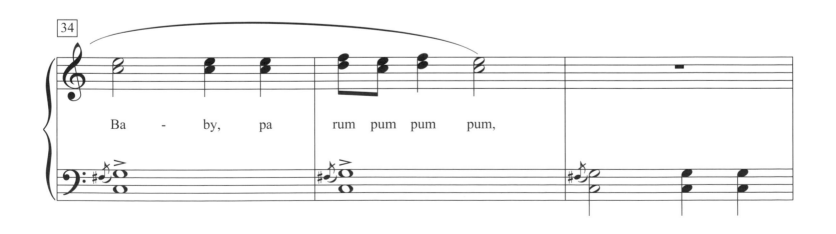

Ba - by, pa

rum pum pum pum,

I am a poor boy, too, pa rum pum pum pum.

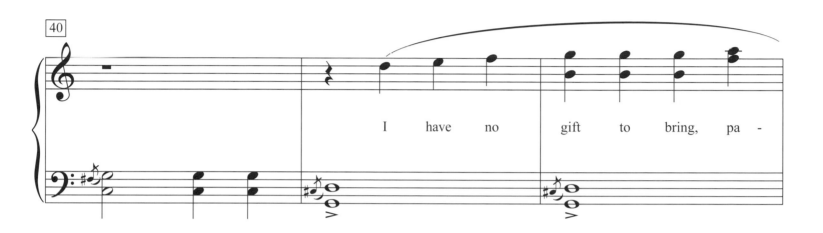

I have no gift to bring, pa -

rum pum pum pum, That's fit to give our King, pa

rum pum pum pum, rum pum pum pum, rum pum pum pum.

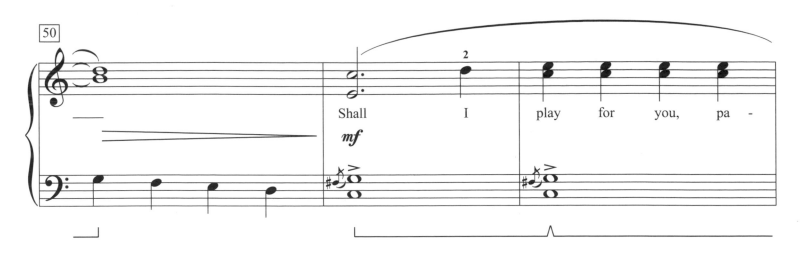

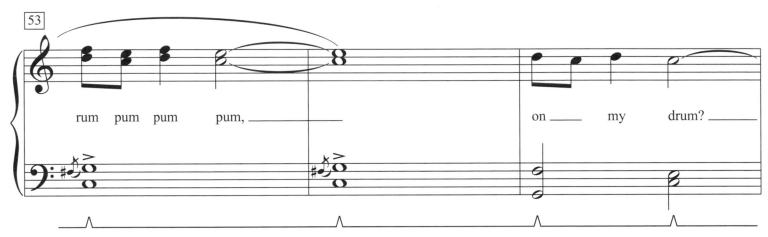

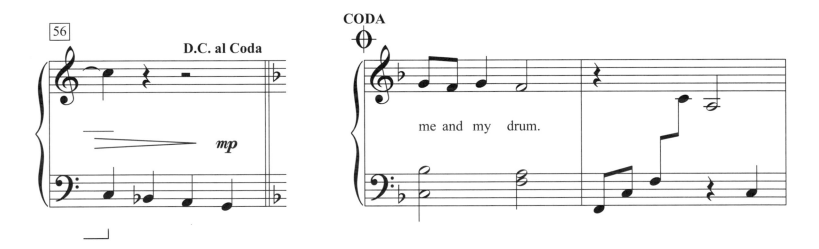

Mary, Did You Know?

Words and Music by Mark Lowry
and Buddy Greene
Arranged by Lynda Lybeck-Robinson

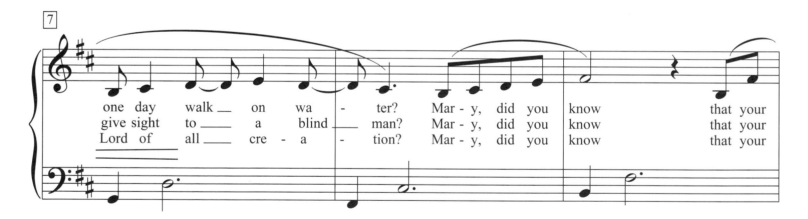

© 1991 Word Music LLC and Rufus Music
All Rights for Word Music LLC Administered by WB Music Corp.
All Rights for Rufus Music Administered at CapitolCMGPublishing.com
All Rights Reserved   Used by Permission

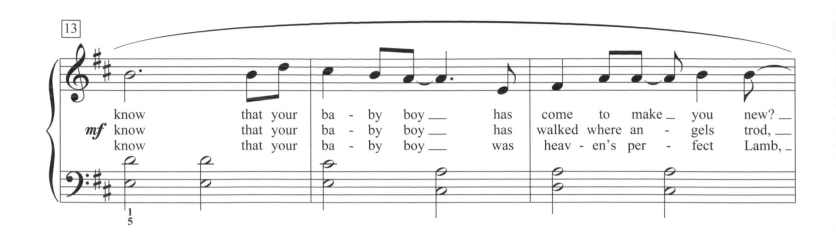

know that your ba - by boy ___ has come to make ___ you new? ___
know that your ba - by boy ___ has walked where an - gels trod, ___
know that your ba - by boy ___ was heav - en's per - fect Lamb, ___

mf

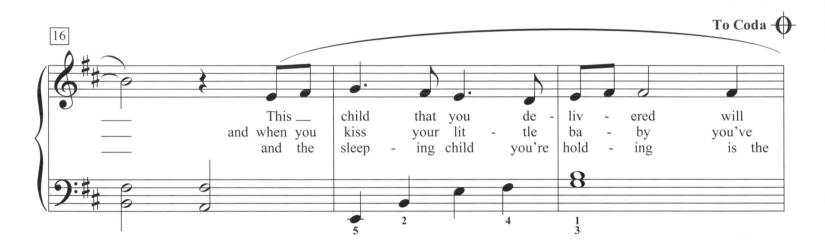

To Coda ⊕

___ This ___ child that you de - liv - ered will
___ and when you kiss your lit - tle ba - by you've
___ and the sleep - ing child you're hold - ing is the

1.

2.

soon de - liv - er ___ you. Mar - y, did you
kissed the face of ___ God? Oh, Mar - y, did you

mp

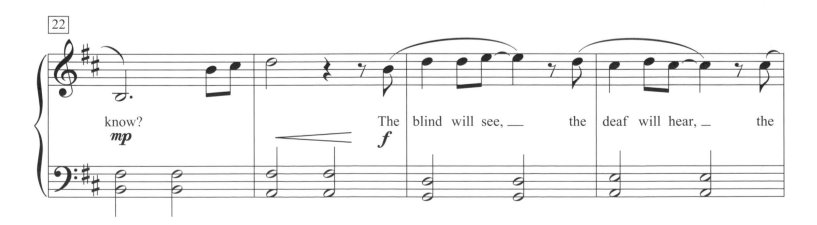

know? The blind will see, ___ the deaf will hear, ___ the

mp *f*

26

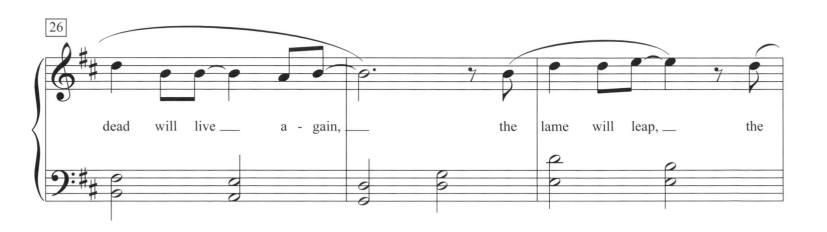

dead will live — a - gain, — the lame will leap, — the

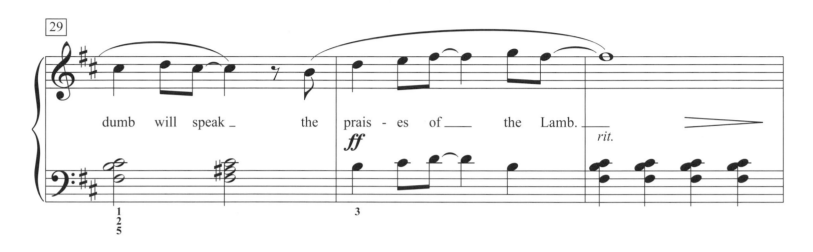

dumb will speak — the prais - es of — the Lamb. —

ff   *rit.*

1
2
5

3

D.S. al Coda

mp   Mar - y, did you
a tempo

CODA

Great

I
f   *rit.*

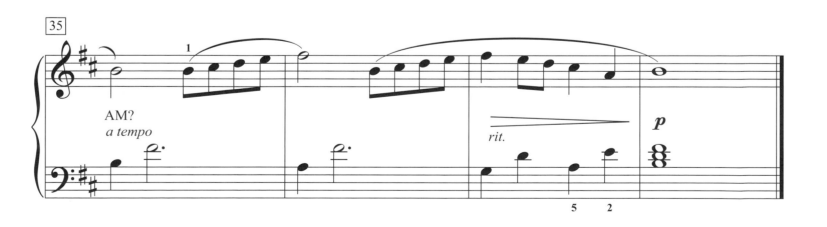

AM?
a tempo

rit.

p

5   2

Sleigh Ride

Music by Leroy Anderson
Words by Mitchell Parish
Arranged by Lynda Lybeck-Robinson

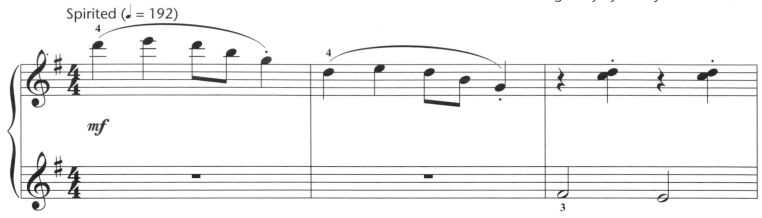

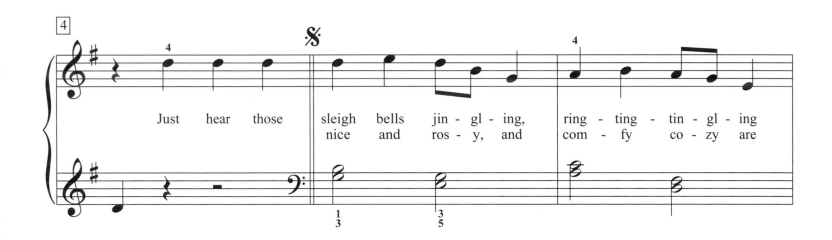

Just hear those sleigh bells jin - gl - ing, ring - ting - tin - gl - ing
nice and ros - y, and com - fy co - zy are

too.
we.

Come on, it's love - ly weath - er for a
We're snug - gled up to - geth - er like two

© 1948, 1950 (Copyrights Renewed) WOODBURY MUSIC COMPANY and EMI MILLS MUSIC, INC.
Worldwide Print Rights Administered by ALFRED MUSIC
All Rights Reserved   Used by Permission

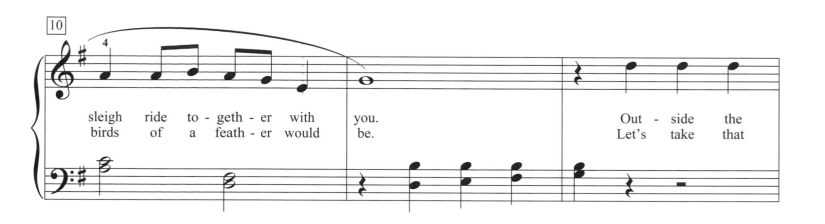

sleigh ride to - geth - er with you. Out - side the
birds of a feath - er would be. Let's take that

snow is fall - ing and friends are call - ing, "Yoo hoo."
road be - fore us and sing a cho - rus or two.

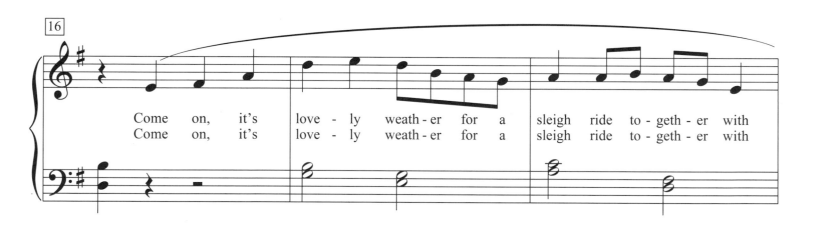

Come on, it's love - ly weath - er for a sleigh ride to - geth - er with
Come on, it's love - ly weath - er for a sleigh ride to - geth - er with

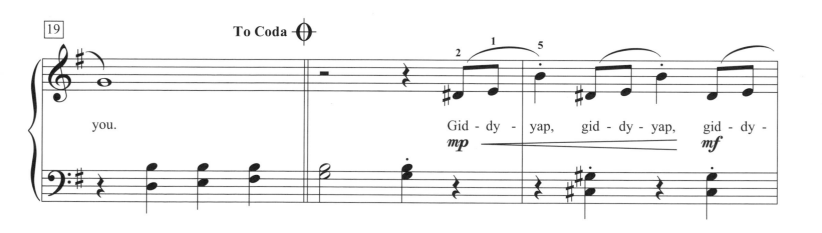

To Coda

you.

Gid - dy - yap, gid - dy - yap, gid - dy -

mp *mf*

yap, let's go, let's look at the show.

We're rid - ing on a won - der - land of snow. _____

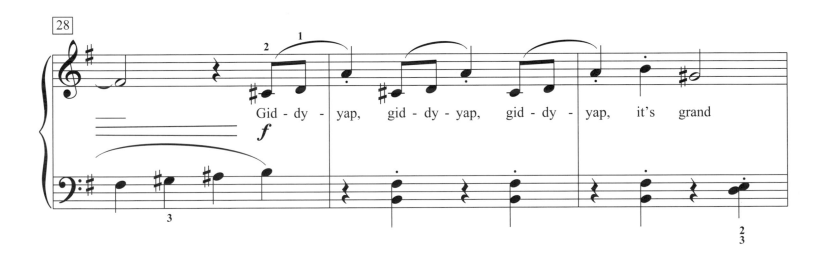

_____ Gid - dy - yap, gid - dy - yap, gid - dy - yap, it's grand

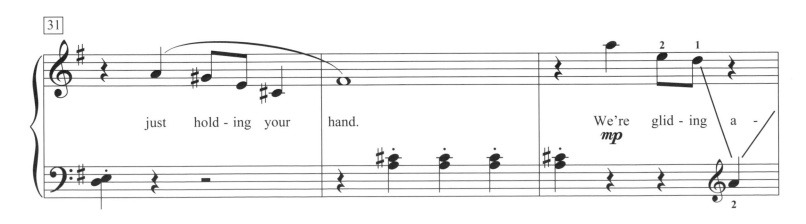

just hold - ing your hand. We're glid - ing a -

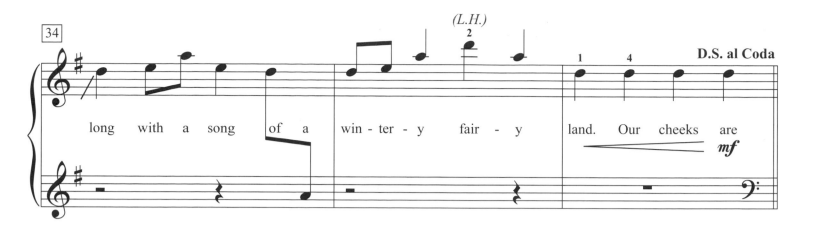

long with a song of a win-ter-y fair - y land. Our cheeks are

Come on, it's love - ly weath - er for a

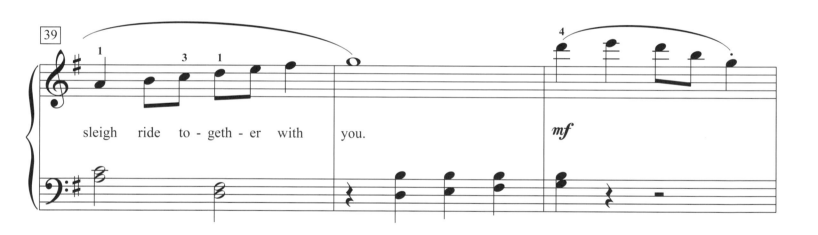

sleigh ride to - geth - er with you.

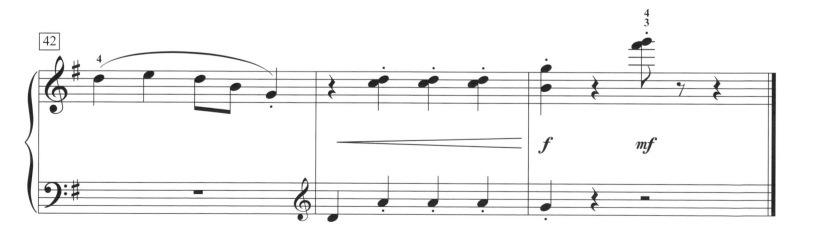

POPULAR SONGS
HAL LEONARD STUDENT PIANO LIBRARY

The **Hal Leonard Student Piano Library** has great songs, and you will find all your favorites here: Disney classics, Broadway and movie favorites, and today's top hits. These graded collections are skillfully and imaginatively arranged for students and pianists at every level, from elementary solos with teacher accompaniments to sophisticated piano solos for the advancing pianist.

Adele
arr. Mona Rejino
00159590 Correlates with HLSPL Level 5..........$12.99

The Beatles
arr. Eugénie Rocherolle
00296649 Correlates with HLSPL Level 5..........$10.99

Irving Berlin Piano Duos
arr. Don Heitler and Jim Lyke
00296838 Correlates with HLSPL Level 5..........$14.99

Broadway Favorites
arr. Phillip Keveren
00279192 Correlates with HLSPL Level 4..........$12.99

Broadway Hits
arr. Carol Klose
00296650 Correlates with HLSPL Levels 4/5.......$8.99

Chart Hits
arr. Mona Rejino
00296710 Correlates with HLSPL Level 5............$8.99

Christmas Cheer
arr. Phillip Keveren
00296616 Correlates with HLSPL Level 4............$8.99

Classic Christmas Favorites
arr. Jennifer & Mike Watts
00129582 Correlates with HLSPL Level 5............$9.99

Christmas Time Is Here
arr. Eugénie Rocherolle
00296614 Correlates with HLSPL Level 5............$8.99

Classic Joplin Rags
arr. Fred Kern
00296743 Correlates with HLSPL Level 5............$9.99

**Classical Pop –
Lady Gaga Fugue & Other Pop Hits**
arr. Giovanni Dettori
00296921 Correlates with HLSPL Level 5..........$12.99

Contemporary Movie Hits
arr. by Carol Klose, Jennifer Linn and Wendy Stevens
00296780 Correlates with HLSPL Level 5............$8.99

Contemporary Pop Hits
arr. Wendy Stevens
00296836 Correlates with HLSPL Level 3............$8.99

Country Favorites
arr. Mona Rejino
00296861 Correlates with HLSPL Level 5............$9.99

Current Hits
arr. Mona Rejino
00296768 Correlates with HLSPL Level 5............$8.99

Disney Favorites
arr. Phillip Keveren
00296647 Correlates with HLSPL Levels 3/4.......$9.99

Disney Film Favorites
arr. Mona Rejino
00296809 Correlates with HLSPL Level 5..........$10.99

Easy Christmas Duets
arr. Mona Rejino and Phillip Keveren
00237139 Correlates with HLSPL Level 3/4........$9.99

Easy Disney Duets
arr. Jennifer and Mike Watts
00243727 Correlates with HLSPL Level 4..........$12.99

Four Hands on Broadway
arr. Fred Kern
00146177 Correlates with HLSPL Level 5..........$12.99

Jazz Hits for Piano Duet
arr. Jeremy Siskind
00143248 Correlates with HLSPL Level 5 ....$20.99

Elton John
arr. Carol Klose
00296721 Correlates with HLSPL Level 5............$8.99

Joplin Ragtime Duets
arr. Fred Kern
00296771 Correlates with HLSPL Level 5............$8.99

Jerome Kern Classics
arr. Eugénie Rocherolle
00296577 Correlates with HLSPL Level 5..........$12.99

Movie Blockbusters
arr. Mona Rejino
00232850 Correlates with HLSPL Level 5..........$10.99

Pop Hits for Piano Duet
arr. Jeremy Siskind
00224734 Correlates with HLSPL Level 5..........$12.99

Sing to the King
arr. Phillip Keveren
00296808 Correlates with HLSPL Level 5............$8.99

Smash Hits
arr. Mona Rejino
00284841 Correlates with HLSPL Level 5..........$10.99

Spooky Halloween Tunes
arr. Fred Kern
00121550 Correlates with HLSPL Levels 3/4.......$9.99

Today's Hits
arr. Mona Rejino
00296646 Correlates with HLSPL Level 5............$9.99

Top Hits
arr. Jennifer and Mike Watts
00296894 Correlates with HLSPL Level 5..........$10.99

Top Piano Ballads
arr. Jennifer Watts
00197926 Correlates with HLSPL Level 5.........$10.99

You Raise Me Up
arr. Deborah Brady
00296576 Correlates with HLSPL Levels 2/3.......$7.95

HAL•LEONARD®
7777 W. BLUEMOUND RD. P.O. BOX 13819 MILWAUKEE, WI 53213

Visit our website at **www.halleonard.com**

Prices, contents and availability subject to change without notice. Prices may vary outside the U.S.